SO YOU THINK YOU CAN
YOU CAN
"GEEZER"

Ben Goode

Published by:
Apricot Press
Box 98
Nephi, Utah
84648

books@apricotpress.com
www.apricotpress.com

ISBN 1-885027-39-7

Illustrated & Designed by David Mecham
Printed in the United States of America

IV

Introduction

A few years ago I wrote a book called, Dr. Ben's Bogus Diet Breakthrough, which was a parody on fad dieting and exercise programs. Even though the material was really good by my standards, it flopped. Nobody bought it. Apparently, people who are dieting don't want to be reminded how pointless and foolish their diet is. And the other grouping of candidates for the book, people who should be dieting but aren't, didn't buy it either for some reason. These risks should have been obvious to me before I ever wrote and published the book and invested a bunch of time and money into it. But I didn't think about them, and since I hate to waste good material I have decided to include a few chapters from Dr. Ben's Bogus Diet Book, that fit into this book when slightly modified, I really want somebody to read it. It makes me laugh. Of course I also wrote a whole lot of fresh stuff that I think is pretty good, too. I hope you enjoy it as much as I enjoyed conjuring it up, and if you don't, please only tell militant feminists and PETA people who have no sense of humor and who never buy my books anyway, so it won't harm my sales.

Thanks, Ben Goode

SO YOU THINK YOU CAN "GEEZER"...

SO YOU THINK
YOU CAN "GEEZER"...

Geezing is not as easy as it looks. It's definitely not for sissies. That's why God made geezers out of people who have plenty of experience and maturity. Those who couldn't handle it he eventually turns into senior citizens, or elderly gentlemen or women. No, geezing is tough. If you can answer "yes" to the following questions, you just might be man or woman enough to be a geezer.

Can you nap 4 times-a-day and still fall asleep in the middle of the 5:00 news?

Can you get up every two hours throughout

the night like pregnant women (and you know how tough they are!) to go to the bathroom?

Can you wake up every morning at 4:30 a.m. and be at your best for two or three hours until you need another nap?

Can you engineer every conversation you ever have into a description of your last surgery or some other health problem?

Can you drive everywhere at half the speed limit?

Can you abstain for years from video games, from listening to any music but oldies and silence, and from caring how you look?

Can you endure regular demeaning visits to the doctor where you are subjected to endless probing and poking--or worse?

Can you get good fragments from most conversations by reading lips or by guessing what people are saying from their body language or hair color?

If you answered yes or no to some of these, or if you want to learn how to geeze properly, or if you want to assist someone else who's trying to geeze, or if you don't really care but your life is so wretched that you need a good laugh, read on…

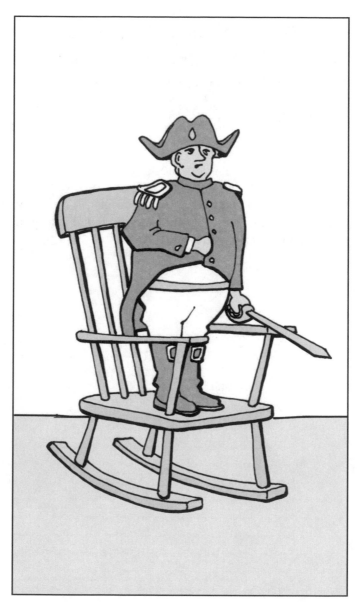

 A REASONABLY
ACCURATE HISTORY
OF GEEZING

Geezing as a popular pastime has been around for a long, long time beginning with Adam and Eve who pioneered the concept of geezing and eventually became the first official geezers having thousands of children who's names they could never get right and ultimately forgetting God's instructions for taking care of the garden and getting kicked out into the dreary world as a result. Only a few hundred years after Adam, along came Enoch and Methuselah who must certainly have had geezing down to a science or something. If they started geezing at age 60 or so, they did it for a long time since they lived to be over 900 years old. Though no record exists, one wonders what kind of drivers they were at seven hundred and fifty or if they could even get a license. Noah was also a geezer. He began a ship building concern at the ripe-old age of four-hundred-and-something, then a sailor after that.

Fast-forward to the year 500 BC. Persian Super king Xerxes was leading his army of 100,000 mercenary troops across western Asia Minor to put down the rebellion of uppity Greek city-states. A few weeks before, he had bought a new hearing aid to take on the trip, and while it worked great in his great hall where acoustics were good and only the accused was allowed to speak one person at a time, out there in the field with horses snorting, armor clanking, and elephants grunting, there was so much background noise that he couldn't hear anything except a cacophony of babble. So, when the messenger came bringing news that a large, spirited force of patriotic Athenians was amassed at Marathon to meet him, and they were armed and dangerous, Xerxes thought he was there to take his lunch order and so he just smiled and nodded his head and acted like he understood. As every school kid who had a superior education in a private school knows, the Persians marched into the Athenian double envelope maneuver and military history...but on the losing side because Xerxes with his hearing loss was obviously geezing.

Some time later in the latter part of the 16th century, English queen Elizabeth was on her throne sweating out the largest maritime invasion in the history of the world. King Phillip, Jacque, or Richard of Spain had assembled his indomitable Spanish Armada and they were poised for invasion. On the eve of the invasion, Phillip thought he would catch the 10:00 weather report just as a last precaution before leaving (and of course the sports final, too.) But as was his pattern, his wife, Mildred, usually had to wake him late at night when the station was off the air, and make him go to bed. So true to form, as soon as his royal backside hit the fluffy recliner with remote in hand, Phillip's eyes closed and he fell asleep in the middle of the college football scores, long before the weather. Next morning, unaware that a huge storm would blow his ships into the British rocks, the Armada sailed off into history. King Phillip was obviously geezing.

It was 1778 and the American Revolutionary war was raging. The British, with their disciplined superior military force had Washington on the run. In fact, General Cornwallis had him cornered near Washington DC and nobody even knew that it WAS Washington DC. Unfortunately, the general was getting on in years and had moments of forgetfulness. Normally the things he forgot were trivial, like the insulin for his diabetes, his pacemaker, or his wife, Blanche, but on this particular occasion, he forgot to bring his navy. As luck would have it, thanks to the cost of the war, the dollar was weak against the euro and so the French were coming in droves to see the Statue of Liberty and Grand Canyon. Since airplanes hadn't been invented, they came in ships and so most of the tours began at the Smithsonian, and since the French were still angry with the British for turning the Acadians into Cajuns after the French and Indian War, the last thing the good, old general wanted to see was a bunch of ships filled with Frenchmen blocking his supply lines and escape route. And so, the British were routed and history was made, and of course, to us today, it is obvious that Cornwallis was geezing.

Not long after that, in 1806 or something, Napoleon was busy conquering the world. And he was having great success and a really fun time. He had had a terrific military education at WestPoint where he learned all kinds of stuff about all sorts of military strategies, not the least of which was the stupidity of starting a land war in Asia. Napoleon scored higher than anyone in the class on the Land Wars in Asia chapter. Unfortunately, by now he was beginning to geeze. This important information was buried in his irretrievably down in his brain underneath the lyrics to a bunch of Mamas and the Papas' songs he didn't even like, a strategy for cheating at golf, and years and years of inconsequential 1950's trivia. For weeks as he contemplated his strategy for invading Asia, Napoleon thought he vaguely remembered something about land wars, but tried in vain to retrieve the detailed information from his tired memory.

Riding home in defeat, having been the cause of the death of thousands of his crack troops and the misery of millions of civilians, finally, the information from years earlier about war in Asia popped into his head during a moment when he wasn't trying so hard to remember it. In fact, it popped into his head as he was chuckling while recalling the time he had released a bunch of skunks into the gym during the junior prom. The obviously Geezing Napoleon cussed his luck.

Of course, today geezing plays a huge part in history, but unfortunately, the rest of the information in my brain is also buried under a few decades of names of "be" verbs, assembly instructions for grand kids' Christmas toys, and the words to every song Barry Manilow ever sang, but you get the idea.

SO YOU THINK YOU CAN "GEEZER"...

HOW TO THINK LIKE A GEEZER

Many younger people have noticed that geezers have a unique view of life. By the time a person gets to be your age, he/she has lived through so many experiences good and lousy, that he/she knows pretty much everything that can go wrong in any situation. So, if you want to think like a geezer you need to pretty much close your mind to doing everything out of fear that something will go wrong. Life can be so simple when the answer to everything is "NO." Besides, it's true that geezers really do know how much trouble doing just about anything can be. For starters, everything-and I do mean everything-costs too much, when compared to 1959 prices, which we still stick to and compare everything against. Cars cost too much so we geezers stick to our 1963 Edsel that's paid for. The gas costs too much so we limit our driving to the post office, the doctor, and to wherever younger people happen to be driving just to irritate them. Motel rooms cost too much so we camp out in our tent or trailer. And of course, computers cost way too much, so we stick to our 1980 Apple with software and printer that is no longer compatible with anything and that can't actually DO anything, but that's not important because we can't actually do anything on our computer anyway because not only are we thinking in terms of 1959 dollars, but we're also locked into 1959 technology including TV sets that just have on-off, vertical hold, and volume.

Unfortunately, there are a few times when a person really does need to get something done. Despite everyone's warnings that you will die if you climb up onto the roof to change the pump on the swamp cooler, you geezer guys still think you can do anything you did when you were twenty-three. So, you climb up onto the roof, tools-in hand, determined to prove them wrong. After un successfully fumbling around for a while with wobbly knees, you climb down in defeat.

Even though you don't know how to text-message on your cell phone, you try for a few minutes to contact your wife before your phone slips from the fingers of your free hand onto the ground. And remarkably, just like when you were a kid and older people warned you not to do dangerous stuff, you do manage to get down alive all by yourself by getting your wife's attention through your squeaking and grunting and tapping with your foot on the window, and when she finally arrives, you still have two fingers clinging to the rain gutter as she slides the ladder underneath your dangling feet. No problem. You just got two years of isometric exercise in just a few minutes, incurred another injured and broken something to give you another topic of conversation—and you found out one more thing to say "NO" to that had been left off your list.

The Look of Youth

Most geezers, when they run into someone from their high school or college days takes a quick look at the person and chuckles to him or herself how glad he/she is that he/she hasn't aged as bad as they have. Ironically, the person being run into is thinking exactly the same thing. This is a strange phenomenon. For some strange reason known only to God, most older people think they look better than other people their age. I ran into one of my old high school classmates and she looked really rough. I honestly thought to myself, "She and her husband look like my grandparents after open-heart surgery. I should probably talk to her because she probably feels uncomfortable because she's probably amazed and a little embarrassed at how young the wife and I look by comparison." Later in the evening I found out the truth through a third party, namely that she and her husband were wondering why my wife and I looked so old (I believe the term, an old saddle" came up somewhere.) and why they looked so good by comparison. Hmmmm. Needless to say, I went to try and find out what had happened to her eyesight and ask a few probing questions and we started talking about her hip replacement and gall bladder surgery. And we found out that she hadn't

13

heard that I had been in the hospital having my kidney stones looked at, which turned out not to be kidney stones after all, but were, in fact, a herniated disk and to make it all worse, they didn't even do anything to fix the problem because I had some ligament damage from years ago that had healed on its own but still caused me some discomfort, and I think I'm pre-diabetic and will probably need gall bladder surgery sometime soon. Since this eye-opening experience, I have had many other peers think they looked better than me, while I assumed they were impressed at how young I looked compared to them, from which I have concluded that many older people are delusional.

So you see. In order to geeze effectively, you should start with delusional thinking like a geezer so there is something you can go to work on right away. If you want to.

Reasons to be glad you're a Geezer...

• *You have been through nearly every kind of depredation imaginable and survived; no money, no job, no food, no TV, no clothes, no friends, no experience, etc., so you know you can handle just about anything.*

• *You are capable of living without your cell phone for more than 24 hours.*

• *You are capable of letting your cell phone ring, beep, play or whatever, without answering it until you're darned good and ready.*

• *You can go for days and weeks without turning on our computer.*

• *You know pretty much everything.*

HOW TO TALK LIKE A GEEZER

To be an effective geezer it's important that a person knows how to talk like one. There is a considerable amount of preparation necessary for most people to learn to speak geezereze Specifically, it takes a very long lifetime of failure, betrayal, illness, and misery to have the experience and paranoia along with the social incompetence to know what to say, and while talking, to be oblivious to the other persons body language when it's obvious to everyone within a 10 mile radius that the listener is trying to gracefully escape the conversation.

In the world of politics, no matter who's elected, whether the economy is booming or recessing, a geezer must be prepared to complain. He must have very strong opinions about every issue that could possibly be discussed even if he knows less about the topic than your average duck knows about calculus, less than most guys know about wedding decorations...even if he has never even herd of bicameral legislatures, checks and balances, and the federal reserve; and then after every lengthy and heated political discussion a geezer must be sharp enough to find a way to engineer the conversation into a discussion about his most recent gall bladder surgery, hematoma, or hip replacement. This is no small order.

Ladies, you, too, must do your homework, because every conversation you have must be laced with references to people long dead or nearly so. You have to conjure up a whole slew of experiences real or imagined that include people with names like "Blanche". Iris, Maude, and Henry and you need to keep a straight face and sound serious and then you need to engineer every conversation around to your hysterectomy, foot scraping, or shunt. You are starting to get the idea and even though your idea may be a little different than my arthritis, I still am having some real problems with my rotator cuff, but I don't really want to have surgery because my insurance won't cover everything and I know Mildred had one a few years ago and it never has healed right and so if she had it to do over again, she says she wouldn't do it again even though her insurance paid everything...

In order to be convincing, both geezers and geezerettes need to polish up their complaining skills-especially about the state of the world and young whippersnappers today because it's entirely possible that they weren't even aware that I went to the doctor, let alone that after the cat scan didn't find any kidney stones because it turned out to be a herniated disc and

18

then when they opened me up and went to repair it they found some torn ligaments that I had lived with for years, and since I had lived with them that long, they decided to just leave them be, and of course they did nothing at all to my gall bladder

Another important tip for up and coming geezers: Be repetitive. Explain the same stuff and be sure to use the same anecdotes over and over and over again. Younger people, especially, love it when you do that. For example, let's say that you have spent most of your life harping on some important principle like, "work ethic." Your children heard about their work ethic daily growing up and nearly everyone you know has too. Needless to say, you are a real stickler with "work ethic." The key then is to introduce the concept into nearly every conversation you ever have. This can be a real problem when the conversation is about how may different family recipes there are for potato salad. For many of us it takes real skill to find a way to turn a discussion about potato salad into a whine session about work ethic, and from there to your gall bladder. But it can be done and it is done millions of times every day by expert geezers. Here is an example: A bunch of people is sitting around the community Fourth of July celebration and the topic of potato salad comes up. Some go on and on about how they love Blanche's recipe. Others comment on how good Iris's is because she uses more yellow mustard with her mayonnaise. If you are working on your geezer talking skills, you can chip in and discuss the fact that the reasons why both salads are so popular is the work that goes into them and how young whippersnappers lack the work ethic to create these wonderful salads because they are lazy and would just go to KFC and buy their salad, thereby depriving the entire community of the diversity of potato salads all because of lack of work ethic. And another offshoot of this is that the nutritional deficiencies in the short-cutted salad most likely contributed to your recent gall bladder problems and will most likely bring down thousands of other gall bladders especially if people don't learn to work harder. See, you can do this!

More reasons to be glad you're a Geezer...

• *You probably won't live long enough to have to pay the national debt the government is racking up.*

• *You can advise anyone because no one has been around long enough to be able to check on your experience or expertise.*

• *During the next war, you won't have to dodge the draft.*

• *You are not expected to look very good.*

• *You aren't in school and don't have to put up with silly professor's class requirements.*

SO YOU THINK YOU CAN "GEEZER"...

HOW TO LOOK LIKE A GEEZER

You're fine pretty much the way you are. Don't change a thing.

SO YOU THINK YOU CAN "GEEZER"...

BECOMING IMMORTAL

One way to tell if you have really arrived as a successful geezer is that people and institutions will name things after you: college buildings, stretches of highway, bridges, wrestling moves, small towns, diseases, etc. Despite my advanced age, for some reason, people seem reluctant to name things after me; therefore, I have no legacy for which I will be remembered and become in that sense immortal. I have always assumed that this would happen naturally when I reached a ripe, old age, but it hasn't. My wife insists that in order for people to want to name things after a person, in addition to being old, a person also has to be rich. This poses a problem for me. Although I am richer than many people in third-world refugee camps, I'm not rich enough to drop a few million into my Alma Mater's scholarship fund.

Rather than settling for only my own little side-

25

walk-brick or concrete square I have come up with a way to increase my odds of having something monumental named after me. I figure that I can start small and build up. If some very minor prominent things have been named after me, maybe I will grow into the role financially of having major prominent things named after me and eventually even maybe be able to get rich enough to consider retiring. So lately I have been naming things after myself. I have started around the house and I figure I will work up from there. We now have the "Ben Goode Memorial Hallway" between the kitchen and bedroom. Our house has a placard on the front announcing that it is the "Goode Building", and our driveway is "The Ben Goode Parking Garage". It's a start.

While I have been trying to tastefully name things after myself, it occurred to me that when I reach full senility my kids will be taking care of me, and since I want to give them some motivation to be rich so they can take care of me in style, I have begun a program of naming things after my kids and grandkids, too. For example, our garden hose has become "River Mandy" after my daughter who is the oldest and will most likely be calling the shots when I am senile. Her husband and my son-in-law have had the septic system named after him: "The Brandon Bates International Water Works." We have named the vegetable garden "Amy Gardens", after my second daughter and the bidet in the master bathroom after her husband; I thought "The Greg Water Park" should flatter him. "Alexander The Gate" is named after my grandson, Alex; the woodpile is "Weswood," after my other grandson, Wes, and "Andon Bridge" is the breezeway that connects the garage to my house, named after you guessed it: my grandson, Andon. The shop/shed out back is named the "Stephen's Industrial Complex," after my son, Stephen, and the walkway into the house is named 'The New Chelsea" Turnpike after my youngest daughter,

There is no end to the possibilities as my family grows. We have houseplants, windows, storage rooms, appliances, you name it. Having something prominent named after me has really changed my attitude. I feel important, even significant. I confident that I am on my way to immortality and big-time success, and respectability. And I'm not even rich--yet.

SO YOU THINK YOU CAN "GEEZER"...

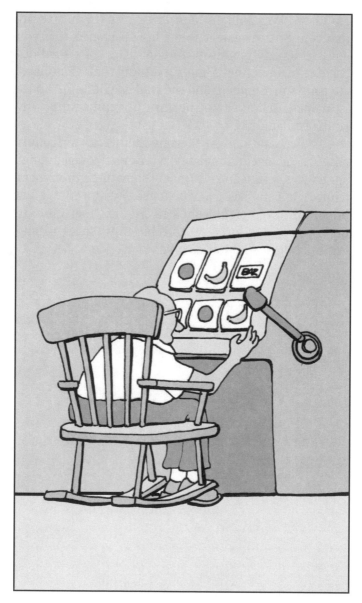

THE MAGIC OF COMPOUNDING

I figure it's not very nice to leave all my readers hanging after that last chapter without helping them gain a solid understanding of how to get rich. Every senior citizen has lived long enough to be a witness to the magic of compounding. You don't need some self-proclaimed financial guru to sell you on the idea that it is THE way to wealth and power. The way the magic of compounding has always worked in your life is this: You put some money in the bank and they pay you interest. Then you pay federal taxes on that interest, then alternative minimum taxes on those taxes. Then you pay state taxes and then local taxes on that same interest until you pull what's left of your money out and pay the same taxes again, and this compounds and compounds until your congressman and a few bureaucrats are set for life with fat pensions for their public service. This is the magic of compounding.

SO YOU THINK YOU CAN "GEEZER"...

For sophisticated investors of larger means compounding has worked for you during your long lifetime on capital investments, too. For example, let's say you are a guy who has invested in stocks, mutual funds, CD's, real estate, commodities, antique vitamins, slot machines, and the state lottery determined to find something that would leave you with more money after taxes than you started with. Sadly most people like me have had some bad luck with our savings and investments. Everything we touch turns to compost. If you get screwed over and over and over again by the financial markets this is known as, "reverse compounding." Or in some cases, "impounding," as in the case of houses and investment real estate and automobiles you bought with money you borrowed. Most geezers I know are experts because of the many experiences they have had with the magic of compounding and impounding. So you can easily see, the magic of compounding on top of compounding, in addition to affecting your mental stability and marriage has a great deal to do with the state of your quest to become financially independent and rich as stink.

Besides just offering you financial security, this concept of compounding can work for you in other ways, too. If you get arrested for speeding and the cop who pulled you over does his computer check and finds out you are wanted for failure to pay child support or DUI and so you are forced to lie about where you got the 100 cartons of cigarettes in the trunk you were planning to sell on the black market to pay your delinquent taxes, which gets you a jail sentence, and while you're in jail your dog dies and your girl friend shacks up with Mel, your former friend, this would be another example of the magic of compounding. In this case it's most likely black magic. When one of your married kids is in financial straits and so you loan him a little money, and then another of your adult kids is facing jail time if he can't get bail money and a good lawyer, and still another one is getting married and wants a blow-out wedding, this is another example of the magic of compounding, which is a real principle that can make you a millionaire over the course of your life...provided that you get a million dollar inheritance or win the lottery.

So keep working on getting the art of compounding down on your way to financial independence.

SO YOU THINK YOU CAN "GEEZER"...

HOW TO TURN A ROTTEN MEMORY INTO A 6-FIGURE INCOME

OK, maybe the title to this chapter is a little misleading. There probably isn't a legitimate way to turn dementia into a 6-figure income, at least if there is, I sure can't remember it, but hey, we were excited and besides, there are some really cool advantages to being older and being able to claim an abnormal amount of memory loss.

For example, if you are over 50, you never have to follow through on any commitment you have made ever again if you don't want to. You can get out of any uncomfortable spot you ever get yourself into by saying "yes" even to hundreds, even thousands of over-lapping things, never mind that you have no intention of ever doing them. Or in the event you change your mind or get a better offer, for whatever reason, you can just flake out and blame it on your bad memory. A wise, old geezer will learn to cultivate this bad memory image so that younger people will come to accept his flakiness.

For many seniors this concept is one of the most liberating revelations they ever have and one of the great rewards of getting older. You are now free to make any commitment you want to any time, even every time, and just do whatever you want to at the moment. You are free in the purest sense. You can promise your daughter to tend her kids and then forget and go golfing. You can promise to be at a Tupperware or some other kind of selling party and then go to dinner with friends and "remember" after it's too late and blame it onto your bad memory. You can even promise to go exercising with a friend early in the morning having no intention whatever to go, sleep until noon if you want to instead and successfully blame it all on your tired, old memory.

I know that some of my more solid, responsible readers are having light bulbs go off all over the place as they begin to put two and two together and realize that some of their ethically challenged younger friends have already been doing this on them. This explains a lot of irritatingly flaky behavior on the part of your geezing friends. Yep. It's also highly likely that you have been conned and hustled by some of your senior friends and relatives for years using this bad memory technique. Don't be upset for long. Just get up to speed as soon as you can and free yourself from responsibility the way they have. Try to get to the point as soon as possible where people are commenting on how quickly your memory has deteriorated. Then you will be free to do anything you want at any moment.

The Name Game

Another good bad memory example has to do with forgetting peoples' names. If you have trouble remembering names, no problem; if you have developed a geezer forgetful reputation, you can call anyone any name that pops into your head at any time and people will just smile and understand. Your children and grandchildren will get used to being called Harvey, and the only punishment you suffer will be watching them roll their eyes. You can even have fun calling your husband or wife any name you want to. A real kick is to pick one name you like and stick with it for a week or two calling everyone you meet Iris or Gilbert until you're tired of it. Then you can switch and start calling everybody Blanche or Burt. I personally have been going with Fred or Luther for either men or women for about 10 years because I honestly can't remember sizzle, but the point is, even if you CAN remember, if you have a few gray hairs, you don't have to. You are free. You never have to stress about remembering names again.

No More Foot in the Mouth

This technique has a million other uses, too. For example, whenever you get on a rant and realize you are about to put your foot into your mouth, you can stop in mid-sentence and claim you forgot what you were going to say. Then, pretend to remember and go off on a completely different tangent. Or if you get too far to stop in mid sentence and you say something you deeply regret, all you have to do is immediately start rambling on about some other totally unrelated topic until you have them confused and baffled or until they forget about the goofy things you said earlier, and are focused on the new topic. You can even illustrate your forgetfulness by bouncing back and forth in sentence fragments and get them totally confused if you ever get yourself into a really tight spot. If you have laid a little groundwork, they will chalk it all up to your wretched, failing memory

Speaking of tight spots, if you are a geezer and ever find yourself being compelled to testify before the senate ethics committee about your criminal activities, or having to explain what you were doing when you ran your Winnebago into the Burger King, you can skip the entire testimony using your geezer memory. If you have laid a little groundwork by being flaky and forgetful because of a bad memory, they will believe you when you say, "I don't remember."

Making Millions

Above I mentioned that there wasn't a legitimate way to make millions and billions using a bad memory. I apologize for my rotten memory. While there probably isn't a legitimate way to make millions using your bad memory, there is a pretty good illegitimate way to do it. The IRS, cable companies, and random law firms have been using this technique for years, using a complicated pass-the-buck bureaucracy as an excuse instead of a bad memory. It works like this: send random bills out to thousands of random people who don't actually owe you any money and see how many will pay the bills. I'm sure there are lots of people out there who will be afraid to get into trouble and who will pay bills they are pretty sure they don't owe and then you can become as rich as the IRS, which is pretty rich I'll bet. If any should call or follow up just do your routine and be the geezer with a bad memory.

One last illegitimate strategy that falls into the category of saving money which is a lot like making money only different is the technique of forgetting to pay your bills. If you should forget to pay all your bills this month, you would have lots of money left over that you can use to buy medication, loan to your married kids, or play BINGO or Canasta. Take a cruise. A penny saved is a penny earned.

SO YOU THINK YOU CAN "GEEZER"...

HOW TO MESS WITH THE MINDS OF YOUNGER PEOPLE

One of the great rewards of living to a ripe, old age is being free and able to mess with younger people. Have a blast. Try some of these methods:

Ask the same questions and tell the same stories and anecdotes over and over and over again.

Give them way too much information about your illness, physical condition, or medical exam.

Pretend to fall asleep in mid sentence and observe how they react.

Try your best to dress like a teenager: sag your pants, wear spaghetti-strapped tank tops, get some piercing and tattoos, etc

Practice really hard until you can beat them at video games.

Ask them a question and then pretend to fall asleep before they finish answering.

Ask them a question and then pretend to fall asleep before they can answer. Wake up and ask them the same question again and then fall asleep again. Play this game as long as you want.

Tell them you're constipated and offer them $20 if they will have a bowel movement for you.

Describe in graphic detail what the doctor does to you during your annual physical exam.

Offer them $50.00 if they will have your colonoscopy for you. Then explain what happens during a colonoscopy. Be sure to exaggerate the best parts.

Pull a badly soiled hanky out of your pocket and blow your nose loudly whenever they come around.

Get huge speakers and play Frank Sinatra while cruising in your car. And turn it up, especially the bass notes until you reach the decibel level of a nuclear explosion, tsunami, or young person's stereo.

Pretend to be constantly text-messaging someone.

Drive at one half the speed limit everywhere you go.

You and your husband or wife can perform a series of passionate displays of affection in public.

Pimp your wheel chair really nice. Beef it up to do wheelies and peel out.

Pimp your walker.

Play your air guitar and sing the lyrics to something by Herman's Hermits or The Monkees as loud as you can.

Wear a Speed-o, bikini or spandex.

Ride a skateboard everywhere you go.

Talk to yourself loudly and be sure to answer loudly a series of health questions.

Announce that you voted for Richard Nixon
and are proud of it.

Announce that you voted for Millard Fillmore.

Announce that you voted for Thomas
Jefferson.

Make up outlandish tales of when you were a
kid and had to catch what you ate, make all
your own clothes, and that you invented TV,

Outfit your fishing raft with wheels, steering
wheel and motor and drive all over town in it

SO YOU THINK YOU CAN "GEEZER"...

10

WISDOM OF THE AGED

For most of us, accumulating bad experiences makes us smarter and wiser all the time. Therefore, it stands to reason that the most brilliant people are very, very old. The problem with me as I've aged is that much useful intelligence has become buried in my brain under stuff as the wisdom, facts, and information until it has piled up to such a degree that I probably pretty much know everything, I just don't know how to get it out of my brain to be put to good use. So, if I were the rest of you, whenever some old guy like myself does successfully pull something out of his brain. You will definitely want to stand up and take notice. With that in mind, here are

SOME IMPORTANT FACTS I'VE LEARNED SINCE GETTING OLD...and which I have successfully retrieved from my over-crowded, very wise brain:

45

Taking blood pressure medication greatly improves ones chances of being arrested for public urination.

You can't automatically assume an older person is hard of hearing or can't hear you just because he doesn't respond; you should also consider that he might also be ignoring you.

There are virtually no places on the human body where hair won't grow.

There are many ways to get even with the younger generation for all the inconvenience, expense, and irritation they've caused you over the years. Driving a car is one of them.

For purposes of senior meal deal prices, 18-year-old order takers usually can't tell the difference between someone who is 39 and someone who is 79, and usually they don't even care.

On the other hand, people over 60 usually can't tell the difference between someone who is 17 and someone who is 27, and they don't care either.

Electronic gadgets rarely work.

Young people are all involved in a conspiracy to fool older ones into believing they can make gadgets work.

There is a conspiracy among computerized gadgets to stick it to older people.

Silence is actually better than most music.

Many people try to irritate older people by

talking softly, mumbling, and in some cases silently mouthing words.

5 A.M. to 8 A.M. really is the best part of the day.

Most people would get much more done and be less ornery if they would just have a nap in the afternoon.

Unlike wine, an old song that was lousy thirty years ago does not improve with age.

Pretty much everyone's parents are really smart. And approaching genius status.

More reasons to be glad you're a Geezer...

- *Either you have enough to retire or you don't. No point in worrying about it now.*
- *You can say pretty much anything to anyone. No one expects you to be diplomatic.*
- *Your grandkids will set up all your electronics, often without you having to get out of your recliner.*
- *You can save lots of money on travel because you have pretty much seen it all, and what you haven't isn't worth the effort.*

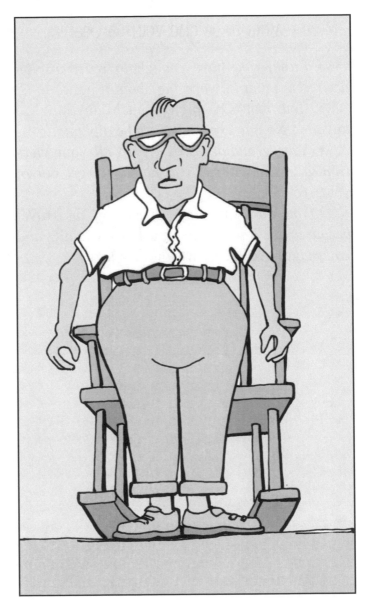

 GEEZING TIPS

This chapter deals with some common age-old problems for nearly all geezers.

The flabby stomach.

For many of us as we get older, our mid sections begin to morph. We have a softening of the muscles around the abdomen combined with an expanding of the solar girth, often called a "prosperity belly." If you are a person who can use a platform sticking out in front where you can set your tools, lunch tray, or chin, then you don't need to read this chapter if you don't want to. On the other hand, if you would like to solve this problem once and for all, you can read on in the hopes that we know what we're talking about. And since the younger generation is getting so soft and flabby there are many of you youngsters who can also use these tips as well.

The problem here is gravity. It causes your belly to sag so it won't support even a low-carb lunch tray or a light chin, and it also causes your pants to fall down around your ankles if you have no belt. Sadly, the laws of physics are most likely here to stay for a while, so let's look at some modifications that don't require that you lose any of your belly or weight. With a large belly, one option is to do as many gangster-wanna-be teenagers do and walk with your legs spread apart trying to look cool while keeping your pants up. While this works marvelously well for millions of teenaged boys it does have the side effect of making geezers look pretty goofy, kind of like a geezer trying to be hip by sagging his pants.

Another option is to wear a belt and put it on top of your stomach or below your belly. If you choose to hike your pants up so they ride on top of your belly you will look like a person who has solved the problem of gravity-sagging belly and pants, but is also a goof-ball. If you're OK with that then read no more. If you would rather choose to wear your pants on the bottom of your belly in an unnatural position facing the floor, the best solution is to have the misses sew a patch of Velcro onto the inside of your pants. This will allow you to take advantage of another of God's gifts to old people: that patch of hair that has been expanding and wireifying on your belly for the past few decades. The Velcro will attach itself to the hair. This will enable you to wear any belt you want and it doesn't even matter if it stares at the floor in apparent defiance of the laws of physics. You can just smile smugly knowing that there is no way your pants will ever fall down. Just try not to think about having to remove the pants and the Velcro in case you ever want to change clothes or take a shower.

SO YOU THINK YOU CAN "GEEZER"...

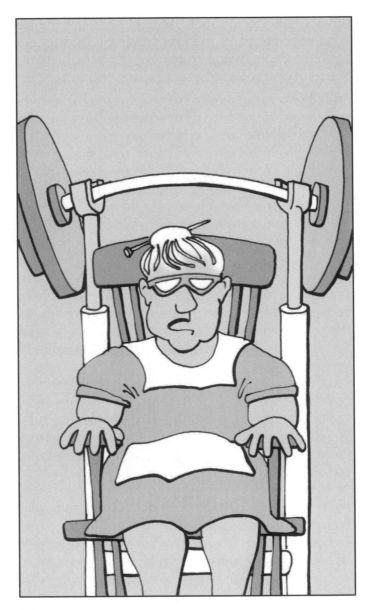

GEEZING IN GOOD HEALTH

One of the major impediments to happy and successful geezing is health. The fact is many people finally reach a financial position to retire and begin to enjoy all the fun things they never had time to do as a regular, responsible adult, when every organ and joint they own goes south and breaks down. Although they finally now have the time, they never get the chance to golf the French Riviera or kayak down the Amazon River because their decrepit bodies have chosen this precise moment to begin decomposing. This book was written so this won't happen to you. Or if it does you can feel your righteous indignation is justified because you know it's not your fault. There are a few secrets to good health as you go older that we would like to share with you. As you know, however, there are many things that we would like to do that we don't get to, such as hanging out with the high rollers and gambling away millions of dollars, having our sweat smell good and, earning a PhD in astrophysics, but since we can't do any of those things, we are going to give you a unique diet and exercise plan that will hopefully make us lots of money. Although it's probable that this program is devoid of any real useful information, at least we have come up with some thoughts that may be entertaining, and we have also come up with a diet and exercise program that is unconditionally guaranteed to work for you absolutely without fail.[1]

Some of you may ask, "Why do we geezers need another diet plan? Everybody from our spouses to our doctors is always ragging on us to eat healthy and get some exercise. There are millions, maybe billions of diet books already out there, and surely one of them ought to do the job." If that one book should surface we won't be embarrassed because we will already have put you on the path to understanding the biggest secrets of diet and exercise, the very road to amazing health and good looks before we actually even get into our amazing program. In fact, let's get the big secret out of the way now so the suspense doesn't give you a stroke or something. Drum roll please...

---

1 We guarantee that not following through on Dr. Ben's Bogus diet and Exercise Breakthrough will get you pretty much the same results as not following through on some pretty famous and expensive diet and exercise programs. Plus, with this particular diet you get the added benefit of being guilt free because nobody expects you to succeed at this one. That's right. There are absolutely no risks here. We promise that when you fail at Dr. Ben's Bogus Diet Breakthrough that's exactly what's expected because you know going in that this is pretty much just a bunch of hooey. You aren't expecting to lose any actual weight, get buns of steel or abs of iron. You can even keep your chins of cellulite if you want. We're perfectly OK with that.

The Secret to Health and Fitness

The number one secret to diet and exercise success, to look slim and healthy all the time: Be born with a naturally high metabolism, solid muscle mass, and long legs. We know this probably comes as no great surprise to those of you with slow metabolisms and short legs that have tried everything from grapefruit rind diets to Himalayan triathlons, but thinking about it can be kind of discouraging. So let's not dwell on it any longer. Sorry for bringing up such a painful subject.

Since we're admitting the truth up front, it should be obvious early on that we aren't trying to sell you another diet and exercise plan that claims it will actually change your life. Just like you, we can't bear the thought of setting ourselves up for another failure. So, the heck with that. Our purpose with the Dr. Ben's Bogus Diet is to achieve fad status so we can make millions of dollars quickly before everything in our diet is proven to kill you.

So, if you're the kind of person who has tried all those other diets before and failed or succeeded for a short time and then ballooned to twice your previous weight, if you are the type of person who likes his or her food, who knows that if you start another diet, you will just blow it again anyway, and who, knowing all that, wants to hang onto some self esteem and feel like you are doing something productive for your appearance and health and well-being, however futile, this diet is for you.

SO YOU THINK YOU CAN "GEEZER"...

THE PARTICULARS OF DR. BEN'S BOGUS DIET AND EXERCISE PROGRAM

Here's the deal: You know perfectly well that with your attitude, you probably have a better chance of single-handedly conquering all stupidity in the world or of curing incompetent drivers on the road, than you do of becoming really fit and healthy.

So it also follows that you probably also stand a better chance of changing the world's popular perception of chubby, un-athletic people than you do of actually becoming fit and healthy yourself. So with Dr. Ben's Bogus Diet Breakthrough, I say we concentrate on the areas where we have the greatest potential for success, and since I'm the one writing the book, naturally I get what I want.

You already know that there are some things you simply are not going to do. For example, you know you should exercise regularly. Every cretin on the planet knows that. You've started over a million times and you've cheated and then petered out a million times more. And so, if you get yourself all psyched up to go out there and try again you know that you're setting yourself up for failure. So, why beat yourself up about it. Face reality. The healthy you with that great body ain't gonna happen. Dr. Ben is OK with that.

You know perfectly well you should change what you eat. Every Bozo on the planet knows he should eat healthy. You've committed to change a million times and you've cheated your way out of that commitment a million times. Time to face reality. It ain't gonna happen. You love unhealthy food. Until now you couldn't even stick to a fad diet long enough to get sick so you could get in on the class action lawsuits that came later. So let's focus on the things that you WILL do. You might as well get some credit for that, don't you think?

TWO THINGS YOU WILL DO

#1 You WILL eat the stuff you like, even sneak it and then lie about it. So let's definitely put that down as part of the diet. You WILL eat pizza, bacon double cheeseburgers, pasta, carbs of all kinds as well as Mexican food, Chinese food, desserts and fully sugared sodas.

#2 You will also worry about dying from a stroke or heart attack or from cancer; you WILL worry about your weight, how you look, and your overall health, at least at the point you start losing it, so let's put that down as part of our diet, too.

It stands to reason that in order to give you the

greatest chance for diet and exercise success, we need to make these two principles the under girding pillars upon which our diet and exercise program is built.

THE TWO MAIN PRINCIPLES OF DR. BEN'S BOGUS DIET AND EXERCISE PROGRAM

PRINCIPLE #1 EAT WHATEVER YOU WANT

PRINCIPLE #2 WORRY ABOUT IT

For the first time in your life, you, my diet and exercise person, are finally standing on the threshold of success. You have a revolutionary program at which even YOU can succeed. Imagine how great you will feel having finally made a diet and exercise program actually work for you. Imagine how wonderful we will feel knowing that we made your success possible and got rich in the process.

CHANGING THE WORLD'S PERCEPTION

When it comes to diet and exercise programs, one other thing we have on our side is the fact that obesity is the number one health problem in the U.S. and the developed world today, and it's only getting worse. So you know there are lots more people like you than there are skinny, fit ones. And I'm here to tell you the skinny, fit ones are nervous as they sense the threat of their political power and popular perception slipping away. I say we organize and use the success of Dr. Ben's Bogus Diet to parlay this political power into a complete change of the world's perception of those of us who are unfit and lumpy. We will get big lawyers to sue and demand that since 70% of the population is obese, 70% of the movies, commercials, and Soaps should be cast with people who are chubby and unhealthy. We as a minority are sick and tired of being disparaged and discriminated against. If a chubby person tries out for the ballet troupe and gets cut, I say we get our mean lawyer to sue on the basis of lumpiness discrimination. If an old flabby geezer like me tries to make it into the Navy Seals or become a Green Beret and gets kicked out, we can sue on the basis of discrimination against unfit people. Think about it. Millions and billions of people out there are not fit and healthy. They have no representation. Changing the world's perception of chubby, unfit people, who take lousy care of themselves, is an important and lucrative pursuit. If the Clintons and Gores can make hundreds of millions of dollars promoting their global warming charity while maintaining multiple high-energy consumption mansions and flying jet-fuel guzzling private jets, certainly I should be able to get in on the action promoting the rights of old frumpy, chubby people. And just imagine, I'm not even a hypocrite doing it. I'm as old, out of shape, and overweight as any of my customers!

FOODS THAT WON'T KILL YOU

Now with that out of the way, let me give you a few great tips on proper eating to make it easier to stick to Dr. Ben's diet and exercise program.

A COMPREHENSIVE LIST OF FOODS THAT TASTE GREAT AND THAT ARE ALSO GOOD FOR YOU:

1.

A COMPREHENSIVE LIST OF FOODS THAT, WHILE NOT SO GREAT TASTING, AT LEAST THEY WON'T KILL YOU:

1. Tofu
2. Broccoli

There. Now go out there and stick to our diet of bacon cheeseburgers and lemon meringue pie. You can do it!

SO YOU THINK YOU CAN "GEEZER"...

HOW TO CHEAT ON A DIET

We at Apricot Press understand that there are many geezers who have an attitude best described as follows: "After all I've been through in my life, I deserve to eat anything I want. I am not going to spend the last few years of my life sacrificing one of my last remaining pleasures, that of enjoying good food just so I can live longer not enjoying good food. You young, vain, fit people eat that nasty-tasting compost. I'll have my sausage and eggs."

Since there are so many geezers out there who are not familiar with Dr. Ben's Bogus Diet Breakthrough and the groundbreaking concepts of eating whatever they want and feeling guilty about it, many of you know, when you tell them you are dieting, they will expect you to avoid unhealthy foods and get some exercise. So, rather than confuse them, if you want to you can go ahead and act as though you are doing a more normal diet where you can't eat anything good. Because those diets really stink, use some of the following techniques to eat the things you want to. You may also want to share some of these methods with other friends of yours who you know are going to blow their diet soon anyway, who are doing more of a conventional diet and hating life.

20 FOOL-PROOF WAYS TO CHEAT ON YOUR DIET

1. Fill your belly button with frosting as you're getting dressed in the morning

2. Feed your dog beef jerky, Spam, Vienna Sausages or something else you like and snitch a bite or two when nobody's looking.

3. Start a food fight and when things get really out of control snag the good stuff out of the air while eveyone else is distracted.

4. At the restaurant, order a salad and low-calorie glass of water, then excuse yourself to go to the bathroom. On the way catch the waitress and tell her it's your birthday.

5. Hide doughnuts inside your pillow at night.

6. Have false nails put on that are made out of pepperoni. Then all day long you can entertain your co-workers as you bite your brown fingernails and swallow them.

7. The bathroom is absolutely the best room in which to hide food. You can claim you're sick and go in there as often as you want, and if you make an occasional animal noise you can stay as long as you want - so long, in fact, that the food you hide in there and sneak can actually have enough time to cycle through. Then you can flush the evidence.

8. Fill your pen with whipped cream or grape jelly. No one thinks twice about pencil and pen chewers.

9. Carry your potato salad-filled shoes as though you were footloose and fancy free.

10. Keep as pets the types of animals you like to eat-a sort of "pet food storage." I'm sure that a halibut would look great in your fish tank and you know that rabbits, pheasants, and turkeys are absolutely trustworthier and make better pets than cats do anyway.

11. Replace your computer mouse with an éclair, PEZ, or Sausage McMuffin and pretend you're having computer problems.

12. Substitute frosting for your toothpaste when you brush.

13. Make up a story that needs acting out in which you use a pizza slice as a prop. For example, demonstrate how the dog bit someone-and that someone can be represented by the pizza. Keep messing it up so you have to do it over and over again.

14. Distract your friends and slip a chocolate éclair underneath the lettuce in your salad at lunchtime.

15. Pick your nose and wipe the wrong finger onto your pants. This leaves the edible protein-based biodegradable material there for you to chew on later if you get hungry.

16. As you fill your blender with your diet protein shake, when no one's looking, slip in a couple of doughnuts or some French fries.

17. Volunteer to take out the garbage, then pause for a while at the dumpster and root around in the leftovers to see if you can find anything yummy.

18. Send pork rinds or twinkies to yourself in the mail. You can often have them eaten before you get from the mailbox to the front door.

19. Wash a cinnamon roll down the drain, then later you can retrieve it by taking apart the P-trap.

20. While jogging, stick gummy worms to the shirt of the guy in front of you. If anyone gets caught cheating on a diet it will be him.

More reasons to be glad you're a Geezer...

• *You don't have to spend good money on new clothes when your old clothes still work fine.*

• *You don't have to come home from vacations until you want to.*

• *You don't have to be discreet; you can say anything you want and blame it on old age.*

• *You aren't expected to do any work because of your bad back, hernia operation, and hip replacement.*

• *You and your wife can sleep in separate beds and no one will wonder if your marriage is having problems.*

SINCE YOU'RE CHEATING ANYWAY...

Since you are cheating on purpose you might as well plan for responses from people concerned about your health and appearance. Here are some explanations you can use to justify why you continue to gain weight even though you're on a diet. These should mollify or at least entertain your harshest critics. Try 'em.

• My doctor tells me I have a body type that absorbs calories from the sheets, blankets, and air around me while sleeping.

• I'm not gaining weight; my friends are shrinking.

• I'm being used for research. They're testing a new medication on me, which is intended to help anorexic people gain weight even if they don't eat anything.

SO YOU THINK YOU CAN "GEEZER"...

• I'm just ahead of my time. The sixteenth century style of chubby, fleshy women is making a comeback. I'm one of the first to get in on it.

• I have had these allergies that are really weird. Every time I sneeze hard, I blow up to the next clothing size.

• These suppository laxatives I take turned out to be Heath bar miniatures. What a bummer. All this time I thought I was purging and instead I was eating Halloween candy.

• Ever since I was hit by lightning my body has systematically begun converting carbohydrates into rare earth heavy metals.

• Aliens are living in my abdomen. As soon as their babies hatch I'll look much skinnier.

• Little fairy monkeys come in the night and slip French fries down my throat every time I inhale.

• I have been constipated for the past three years. My body refuses to let even one calorie escape.

• Last week my wife shaved my back and then oiled me down with some exotic massage oil she found in an Arabian flea market. About 5 minutes later my whole body, except for my ear lobes, swelled to three times its normal size. By the time the paramedics could shoot me full of steroids, I had developed an unnatural attraction to olives, which I have been eating by the handful ever since-especially the green ones stuffed with pimento. The good thing about the whole incident is that the exotic massage oil spilled onto a blanket which now floats around about three feet off the ground, which I use to get around until the swelling goes away.

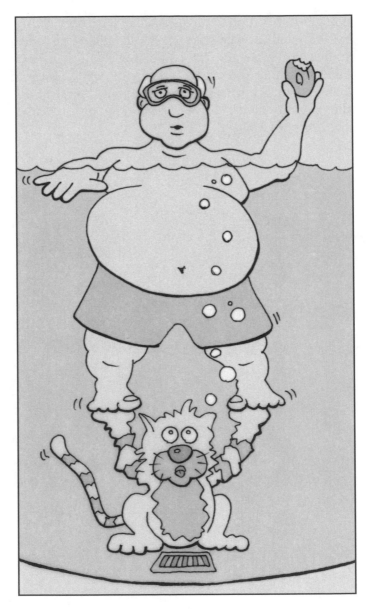

DR. BEN'S BOGUS
EXERCISE PROGRAM

Exercise is a very controversial topic. Some of you veteran geezers get your exercise scratching under your armpit or coughing up a phlegm ball. This will not get it done. In this day and age we're all supposed to have buns of steel and a six pack along with face lifts keeping us looking like we're 18 well into our eighties. Besides, we all know perfectly well that if we don't improve our cardiovascular health quickly we are likely to die tomorrow or sooner from a stroke or from arteriolosclerosis...or even worse, remain alive and looking like a bag of rocks in our spandex or swim suit. This is why I recommend that you take your exercise seriously and this is why this chapter is in this book.

Now, when I say take your exercise seriously, I don't necessarily mean that I expect you to do any actual exercise, at least no yet. If you have been sedentary for a few decades it's best to go slowly and not rush into anything. One guy I know started exercising after a couple of millennia of sitting around and his hemorrhoids exploded because the arteries and capillaries feeding them had calcified into marble. So what I mean by taking your exercise seriously is just what I said. Whenever you think or talk about exercise have a very serious look on your face, kind of like the look on the face of an animal rights activist when you explain to him some of the many ways to skin a cat. So while you're being very serious about your exercise I'm going to share a few of my thoughts on the weather.

As many of you know, out here in the West the weather is unpredictable. Those who have the greatest understanding of this fact are those who are trying to predict the weather, the local meteorologists. (These are they guys who should be out there looking out for meteors or something.) They know from experience that they are probably going to screw up their weather predicting most of the time and so it looks to me as though they have a strategy for hedging their bets professionally. They cover all their bases. If you go to one weather web site and look, it will tell you one prediction, and if you look at another site, that one will predict something else. This system is terrific because with every kind of weather known to man predicted on at least one site, at least one meteorologist is bound to be right at any given time. An added benefit of this type of weather-predicting strategy is that it leaves you, the weather-consuming public, to prepare for virtually anything imaginable. In fact, it can also save you time because you know that going to the trouble to look at the weather websites is pretty much a waste of time because you know that the information is basically worthless, and so you save yourself time by preparing for every conceivable possibility. Take your sunscreen along plus your umbrella, plus your swimming suit, plus your heavy coat and gloves, and a good insurance policy.

This strategy is something Dr. Ben recommends when it comes to your health and exercise as well. Because you never know when your tattered, old body is going to have something break down. Be prepared for anything. For example, some people I know devote countless hours each week to working out. This class of people assumes that their body weather, so to speak, will always be fair and sunny. Sadly, if all they ever do is prepare to be healthy and fit, they leave themselves unprepared and vulnerable when their physical weather changes to sick-o, lazy, or dead. What if in the middle of their exercise regimen, the old obesity bug bites them hard, and all of a sudden they become so large and heavy their joints can't take the pounding caused by walking on the pavement. I know about this. It happened to me. What if some exercise buff is going along doing a regular workout and all of a sudden some disease like gout, plague, or sleeping sickness attacks and he or she can no longer do it?

This is why, just like the meteorologist, we recommend that you hedge your bets. If you want to work out a little, feel free but don't put all your eggs in one cement mixer. Don't just beat around that one fudge brownie. Be sure and plan for the possibility that you might be unable or unwilling to exercise for a few decades. That's why Dr. Ben has a revolutionary exercise program. We're not going to risk telling you to go out wearing only your bikini or speed-o and then have a snow storm move in, metaphorically speaking, and bury you under four feet of ill health. Be sure and take your exercise program very seriously, but at the same time, plan for attacks of inactivity, illness, and stupidity. That way you have all your bases covered.

DR. BEN'S EXERCISE PROGRAM IN 2 EASY STEPS

STEP ONE: WHENEVER YOU'RE REALLY IN THE MOOD, DO A MODEST AMOUNT OF EXERCISE IF YOU WANT TO, OR ELSE DON'T.

STEP TWO: REPEAT STEP ONE.

Note: Most diet and exercise programs give you only one side of the debate: theirs. One of the other unique things about Dr. Ben's Bogus Diet and exercise program is that in an effort to reduce liability, we try to anticipate some of our opponents' thoughts. So we present both sides. We want to be fair. So in a spirit of cooperation and absolute fairness, we give you the other side of the exercise argument. Here go some pretty good excuses for not exercising, which you really ought to consider before you start Dr. Ben's revolutionary breakthrough.

• At your age you probably won't live long enough to make all the effort and sacrifice worthwhile before you die anyway.

• Some person you know (a good friend, relative, enemy, whatever) completely obsessed and knocked herself out getting into shape, exercising for hours-a-day and avoiding tasty foods for decades only to get hit by lightening just as she was approaching her ideal weight and fitness. You are determined this won't happen to you.

• You have lived a very long time. You know that this fitness craze is just a fad. By observing Italian Renaissance art, anyone can see that throughout much of history, being chubby was a sign of beauty, wealth and prestige. Since all of us geezers are witness to the fact that every fad and fashion manages to cycle back around every few years, I'm going to wait until I can get in on that fourteenth-century chubby fad again. I can be patient.

• If a person gets too much friction on his butt cheeks or where his legs rub together, there is a statistically significant risk that a person's hemorrhoids could explode or burst into flames.

• One needs to maintain all the mass one can in order to help his pickup truck get good traction.

• Unfortunately, you are a person who is allergic to your own sweat.

• With all the starving children in Africa, you can't bear the thought of wasting all those perfectly good calories just burning them all up for no good reason.

• You know you would only blow it anyway.

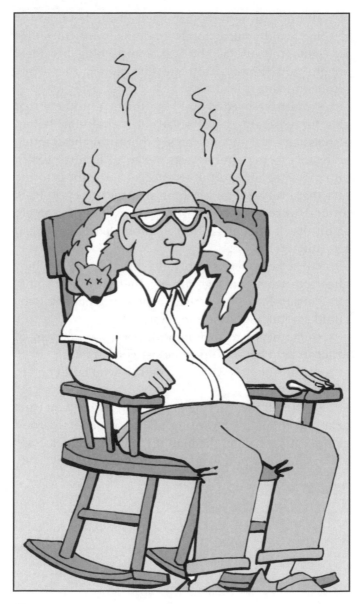

17

HOW TO
ENCOURAGE PEOPLE
TO GO AWAY

There are way too many annoying people in this world: Howard Stern, the guy on the computer commercials with the over excited, but whiney voice, Eunace, Henry, Jackie, and Frank, just to name a few. It may surprise you, but even though I am a well-known writer, I am still constantly badgered by annoying uninvited guests: tax collectors, collection agencies, the CIA, credit card companies, loan sharks, the mafia, the gas company, an annoying neighbor kid, my college-aged kids needing money. Until now, there was simply nothing I could do about it. But, finally, thanks to some revolutionary thinking, we no longer have to put up with annoying people bugging us. Once you've read this piece, never again will you strain to be polite all the while hoping some obnoxious person would go away and let you get your important work done. Never again will you bang your head against the blade of giant earth moving equipment or gnash your teeth against the thigh bone of a prehistoric sloth while you listen to some lame sales pitch for the 800th time, and most likely, never again will you believe much of what I write, because finally, we have this entire long list of solutions to your problem of how to make annoying people go away. Some of these may really work.

21 WAYS TO MAKE PEOPLE GO AWAY

1. Hang a dead skunk around your neck.

2. Make signs that say, "Anthrax Quarantine Area" and put them all over your property.

3. Pull off the road and appear to need help.

4. Wear a hockey mask and carry a chain saw everywhere you go. *Note: this may not deter unwanted phone calls.

5. Make it your practice to hit up everyone you talk to about joining your network-marketing group.

6. Wear bloodstained bandages on your head; better yet, cut an artery and bleed profusely.

7. Powder your face white and wear a black cape.

8. Always carry a supply of religious pamphlets and aggressively hand them out .

84

9. Eat nothing but onions garlic, salsa, and beans.

10. Lie down on the sidewalk and look sick or dead.

11. Wear a Lakers shirt and wander around bragging about how dominating Kobe is.

12. Maneuver every conversation around until you are discussing your health problems.

13. Drool.

14. Be obnoxiously cheery and grin all the time.

15. Whenever asked a question, bark your answers.

16. Never allow an opportunity to ask for money pass you by.

17. Use Scotch tape to tape up your nose so everyone can see up your nostrils clear into your brain.

18. Wear a turban and carry a jar with white powder.

19. Allow your nose to run and never wipe it.

20. Wear a Smurf costume.

21. Put the word out that you're looking for volunteers to help you raise money for the Boy Scouts.

'The Truth About Life' Humor Books